Lost
Civilisations

Lost
Civilisations

Liz Miles

Collins

Contents

Three civilisations 2
Chapter 1 The Indus Valley 4
Chapter 2 Toys, toilets and unicorns 16
Map of the Indus Valley 28
Toys and games 30
Chapter 3 Ancient Egypt 32
Chapter 4 Pictures, numbers and
  unsolved mysteries 44
Map of ancient Egypt 56
Ancient Egyptian animals 58
Chapter 5 The Inca empire 60
Chapter 6 Food, gold and missing treasure . 70
Map of the Inca empire 80
Food 82
Are these civilisations really lost? 84
About the author 86
Book chat 88

Three civilisations

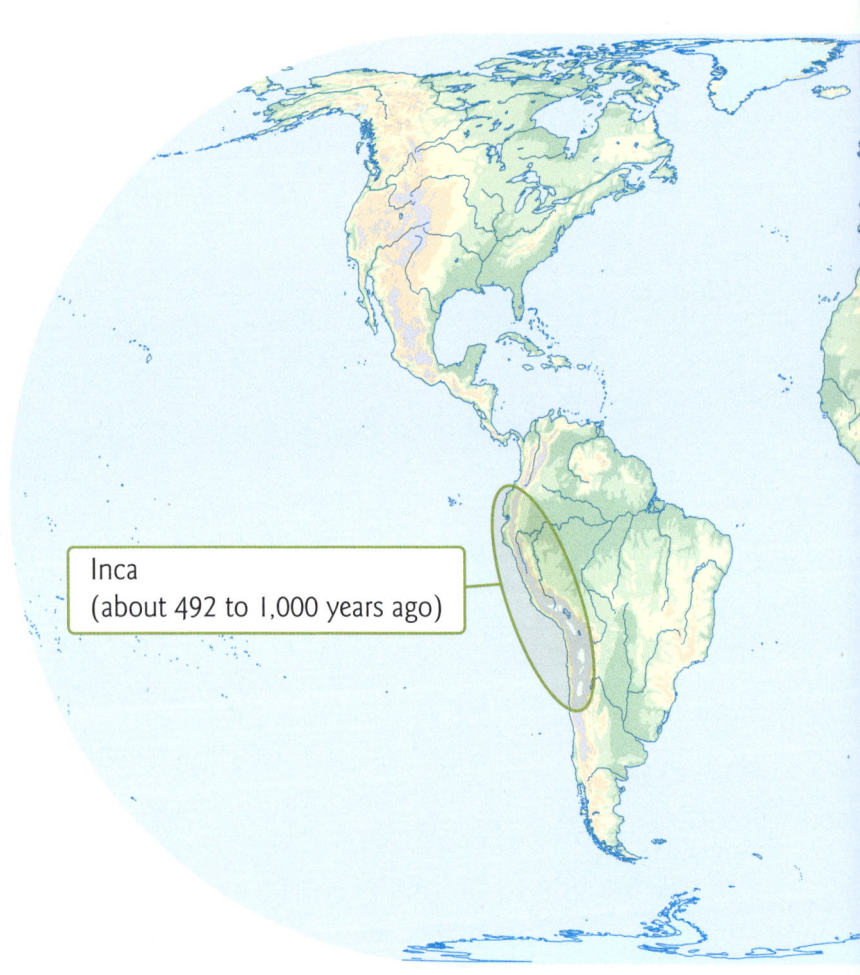

Inca
(about 492 to 1,000 years ago)

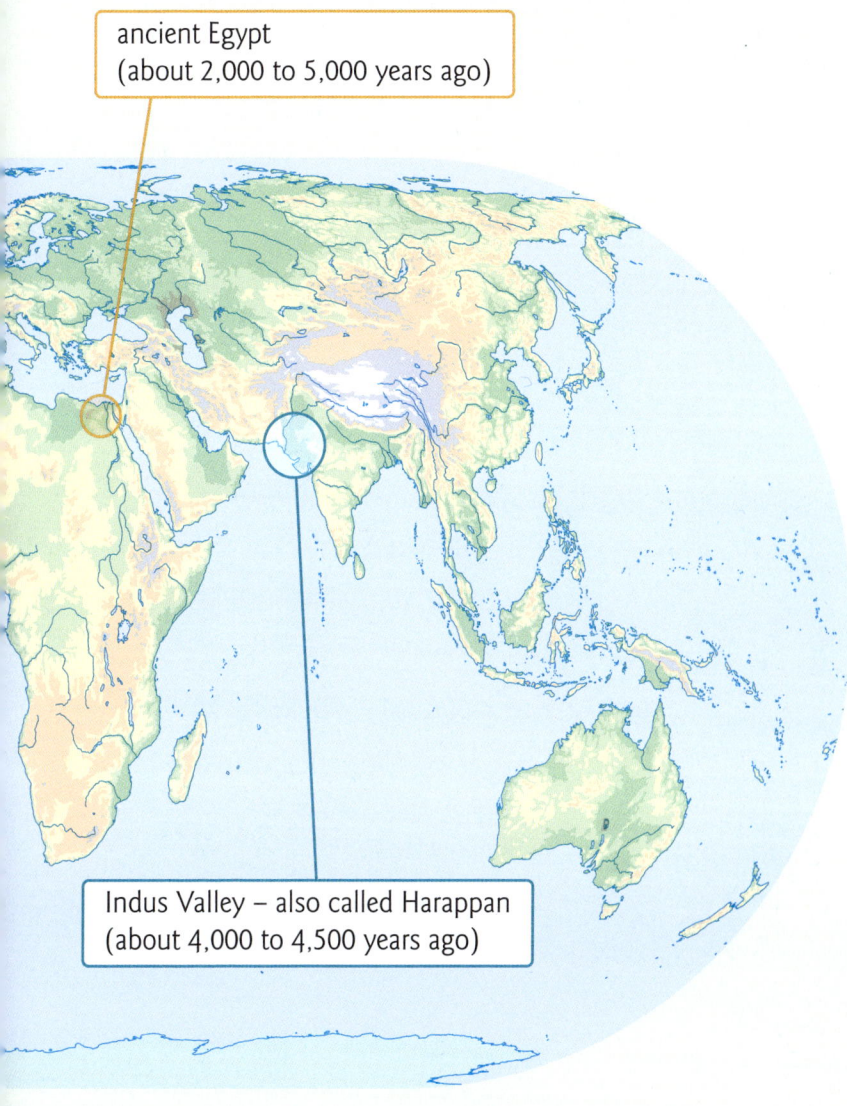

Chapter 1
The Indus Valley

If you time travelled back about 4,500 years to the Indus Valley, you'd soon be busy! Indus children had to learn how to hunt for food, farm the land and make things such as vases or bricks. Some children went to school too, for lessons in reading and writing.

Your home might be in a village, a town or perhaps a city. Exploring one of the fascinating cities would be an incredible adventure – but you would need to be careful not to get squashed by an elephant!

The Indus people lived 4,000 to 4,500 years ago. Many of them lived beside the Indus river, and used the river water to grow food, drink and wash. They also travelled in canoes and rafts along the river. The river came down from the Himalayan mountains, bringing silt – a type of soil that is good for growing plants.

An Indus Valley town might have looked like this.

When historians talk about a civilisation, they mean a large group of people who share the same culture. Culture means customs and traditions. Some people prefer to say 'popular culture' instead of 'civilisation'.

Where did they live?

Many people lived in the city of Harappa in the Indus Valley. But the Indus Valley civilisation spread far beyond this. Archaeologists have found objects made by Indus Valley people in parts of what we now call Afghanistan, Pakistan and India. That's an area around four times the size of the UK.

Around five million people lived in more than a thousand settlements, from villages and towns to big cities. The cities, such as Harappa and Mohenjo-daro, are among the oldest in history.

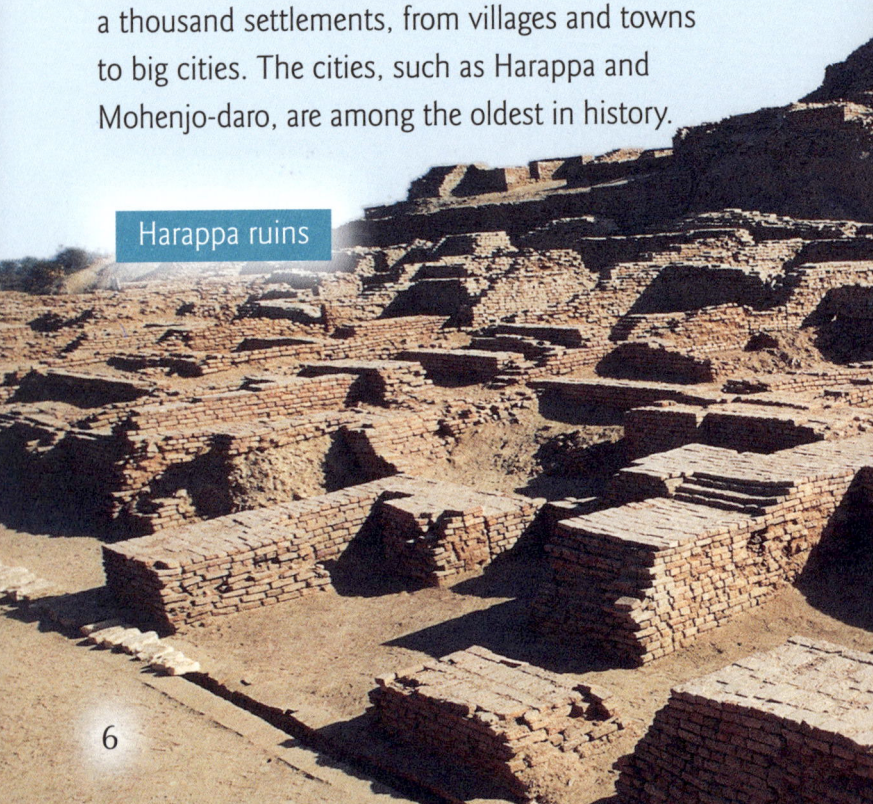

Harappa ruins

The surprise discovery!

In the 1920s, people building a new railway line along the Indus river valley found thousands of similar-sized blocks. Thinking they were just a load of old thrown-away bricks, the workers used some to build the railway. Then they found some stone carvings, so archaeologists checked the area. Those old bricks and carvings turned out to be from the ruined Indus Valley city of Harappa.

> Archaeologists study ancient peoples by looking at what they left behind.

City ruins

The Indus people didn't have computers, machinery, windows or concrete but they managed to plan, design and build well-organised cities. The ruins they left behind show that they used a grid system, with a main road going down the middle, and groups of houses in blocks.

Mohenjo-daro ruins

The main street of the ruined Indus Valley city of Mohenjo-daro was just wide enough for two elephants or two buffalo carts to pass each other.

As well as houses, the Indus people built meeting places, including baths (a bit like swimming pools). Everyone had fresh water, too. They made strong brick wells for every house or group of houses. Some of the wells had ropes and pulleys to lift up the water, and others had steps down to the water.

Wells provided cool, clean water from underground.

The ruined cities show just how sophisticated the Indus civilisation was. While the Indus people were making brick-built, complex cities, people in what we now call England were only building small groups of simple homes.

The grid system of Mohenjo-daro is a bit like modern-day Hong Kong's grid, although it was built over 4,000 years before.

City walls

When people see that Indus cities like Mohenjo-daro are surrounded by high walls, they think it's a sign that the cities came under attack. In fact, it's likely that the walls kept the cities safe from floodwater rather than any enemies. Experts think the Indus people didn't have armies because they haven't found many weapons.

Food and water

Thousands of people lived in the settlements, and they needed a reliable supply of water and food. Archaeologists have found channels dug into the ground which moved water from the river to fields. Reservoirs like this one stored water ready for dry weather.

In rain storms, drains stopped the reservoirs from overflowing.

Indus grain house (granary)

The Indus people built granaries to store their grain, too. This meant that they had a way to store food for use all year round.

Selling and buying

Most Indus people didn't live in cities. Instead, they lived in places where they could work on the land as farmers, or in mines, digging for metals or precious stones. Lots of people spent their time making things they could sell, too. To sell what they'd grown, mined or made, they probably travelled to a city market.

Ancient logos

Companies today often print their company name or logo on things they sell. It proves they made them, which helps customers know whether they are top quality or not. Guess what? The Indus Valley people had already come up with a similar idea: seal carvings. Each carving stamped onto goods proved who the seller was. Lots show animals, so these are a clue to the types of animals they often saw. Most include Indus writing, too.

These are elephant and bull seals with Indus writing above.

Found far away

Some things made by the Indus people, like vases and jewellery, ended up a long way from the Indus Valley. They crossed the Himalayan mountains and the sea, and reached places like modern-day Oman. This shows that, just like today, Indus people liked to trade – sell, buy or swap things – with people who lived far away.

Carved gemstones like these, from Mohenjo-daro, were found far away in Oman.

Chapter 2
Toys, toilets and unicorns

The Indus Valley civilisation left behind all kinds of things that tell us how they lived. These are all clues about their culture – what they ate and wore, their craftwork and even how they had fun. Remember, powered machinery didn't exist then, so everything was made by hand.

Toys

Did Indus children have toys to play with? The answer is almost certainly, yes. Objects like model boats, little animals and bird-shaped whistles that have been discovered are probably toys. Puppet-style figures include a model monkey designed to climb a string and a cow that could nod its head. Dice show they played board games. Most of the toys are made from clay.

This object might be a simple toy puzzle, like a maze for a small ball like a marble.

Toys like this give us an idea of what life-sized carts might have been like.

Figurines and fashion

Figurines (small statues) can tell us a little about what people enjoyed doing and what they looked like.

Some experts think one important bronze figurine shows a woman dancing, so perhaps dance, music and singing, were important to the Indus Valley culture.

This standing figure tells us that some women tied their hair back in a bun.

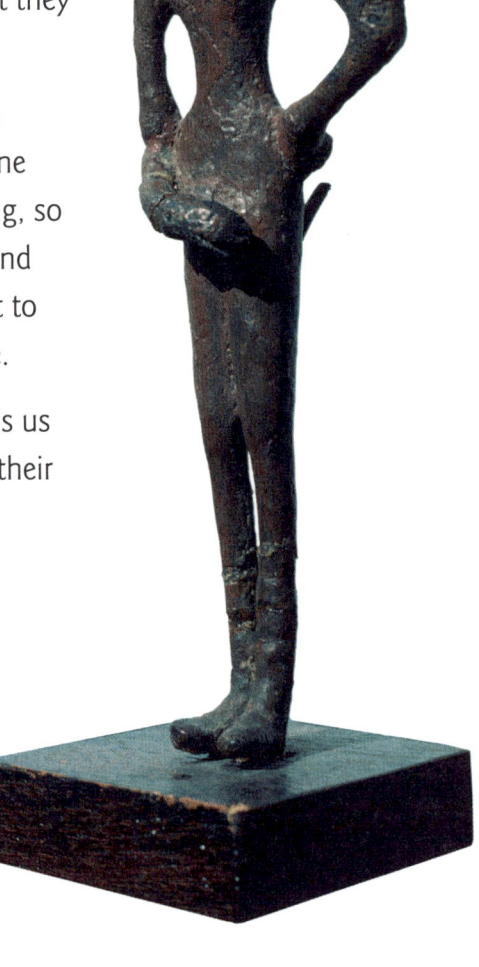

Some of the Indus Valley figurines show how skilled the makers were. This carved stone figure is often described as a king or priest but there's little evidence that the Indus people had kings or priests. It's more likely to be a leader or other high-ranking person. His beard and patterned robe give us clues about Indus fashions.

The craftspeople made beautiful jewellery, and the pieces found in graves show that both men and women wore jewellery, such as necklaces and hair ornaments. These bangles and earrings are made from conch shells and gemstones.

Thanks to the Indus Valley people

The Indus Valley people carefully planned and built cities with brick buildings and roads. They left behind many other ideas, too. It's possible that they were the first to come up with the following ideas.

Drains and flushing toilets

Dirty water and floodwater can cause illness, but the Indus people carefully planned how to channel this away. Small drains from houses and roofs carried water to main drains in the street. There's even evidence of inspection holes – where workers could check the drains for blockages.

a brick drain

In towns and cities, houses with yards had a place to wash and a hole for going to the toilet. After using the holes, people flushed them by pouring a jar of water down. This is the earliest example we have of a flushing toilet!

a tunnel for sewage (toilet waste)

Litter

Rubbish was left behind in small areas of Indus cities. This suggests that people carefully put their rubbish in particular places for collection.

Weights and measures

As far as we know, the Indus people invented the first system of standard weights and measures. This system meant that everyone knew exactly what they'd get if they bought a certain amount of grain or a certain size of jar. It made selling and buying much easier – it was easy to prove if a bag of corn was too small.

By inventing tools to measure length, they could also make sure things matched. Using bricks with the same dimensions made it much easier to build things. Imagine how hard it would be to build or mend a wall with bricks of lots of different sizes.

scales and weights from Mohenjo-daro

modern scales and weights

Buttons and tiles

Buttons are a small but important Indus Valley invention. Indus people used buttons mainly to wear as ornaments, rather than fasteners. Their buttons had lots of different designs, and some might have been used like the seal carvings, to stamp on things they owned.

The tiles found in the Indus Valley still inspire us today. You can see geometric shapes, animals, and shapes inspired by nature in their designs.

Unsolved mysteries

Lots of puzzles and mysteries surround the Indus Valley civilisation. There is still a lot to learn about how they lived, and we haven't been able to translate their writing system. These are some of the many mysteries that experts are still trying to solve.

The puzzling code

No one has worked out what the picture-signs in the Indus Valley writing system mean. So we don't know whether there were any leaders or laws, or how decisions were made. We don't even know what language they spoke.

Indus writing looks like picture-signs or symbols.

Instead of pens and paper, Indus Valley people drew the picture-signs on clay with a stick, carved them on stone or scratched them onto metal.

They left their mysterious writing on seals, clay tiles and metal. The longest piece of writing that's been found has about 26 picture-signs. Perhaps, one day, computers will help experts to work out their meaning.

Is it a unicorn?

Some of the seals appear to show a one-horned animal. Is it a unicorn or is it a two-horned animal viewed sideways, so you can only see one of its horns?

Why did the civilisation disappear?

No one knows for sure. The people might have moved on because the climate became too dry, and rivers dried up. Some experts think heavy rains caused a massive flood. Other experts think a travelling tribe drove them away.

> The cities of Harappa and Mohenjo-daro were given these names after the ruins had been discovered.
> The original names are still a mystery!

BONUS

Map of the Indus Valley

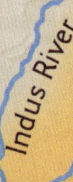

Indus Valley Civilisation

Mohenjo-Daro

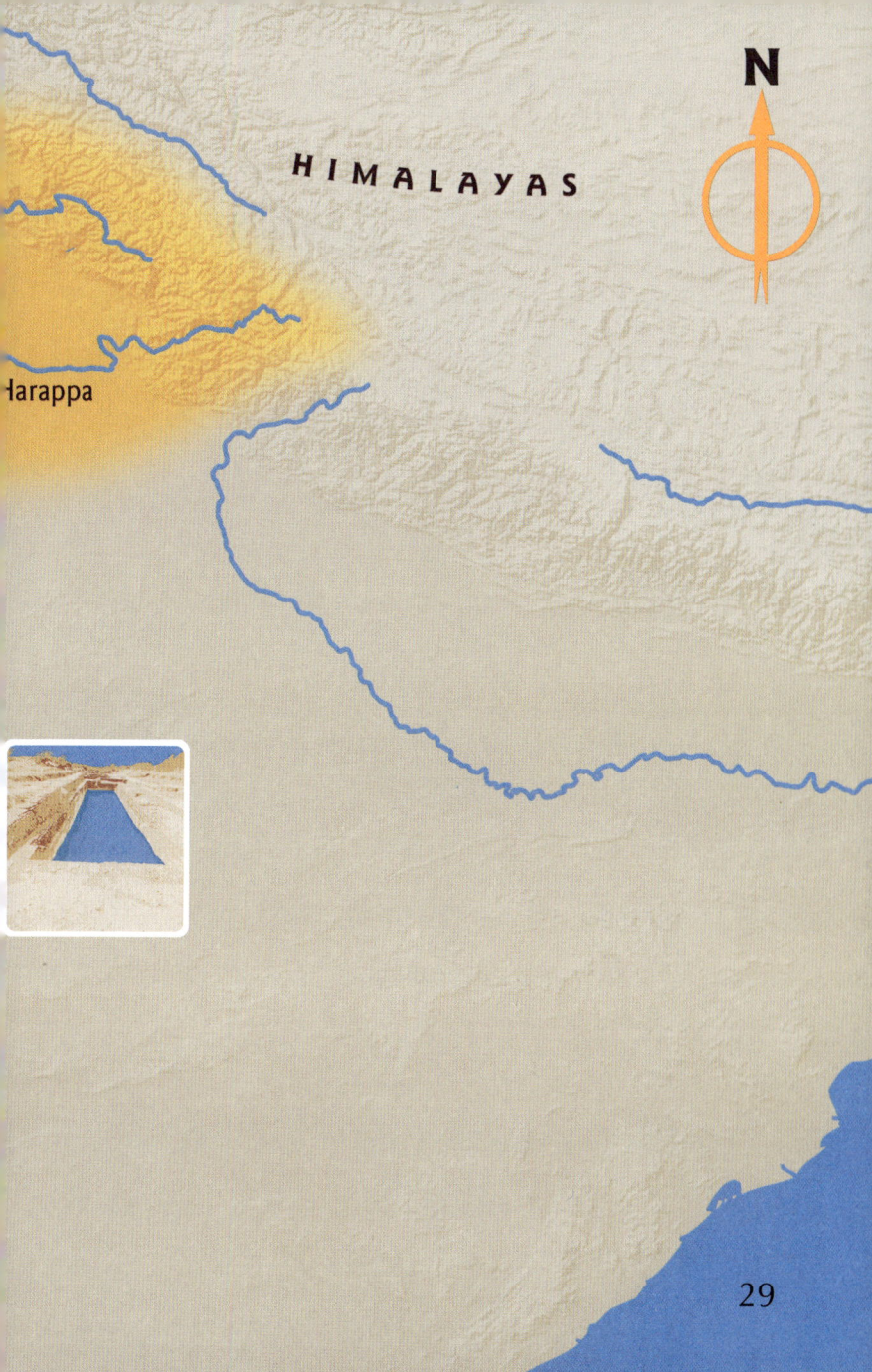

Toys and games

Lots of past civilisations left toys and games behind. Some of ours are quite similar!

This 'Royal Game of Ur' is from a civilisation called Mesopotamia. The first to get all their pieces to the end wins!

Some experts think that the Indus Valley people invented dice. These are from Mohenjo-daro.

The game of 'Go' was invented in ancient China. To win, your stones must gain the largest part of the board.

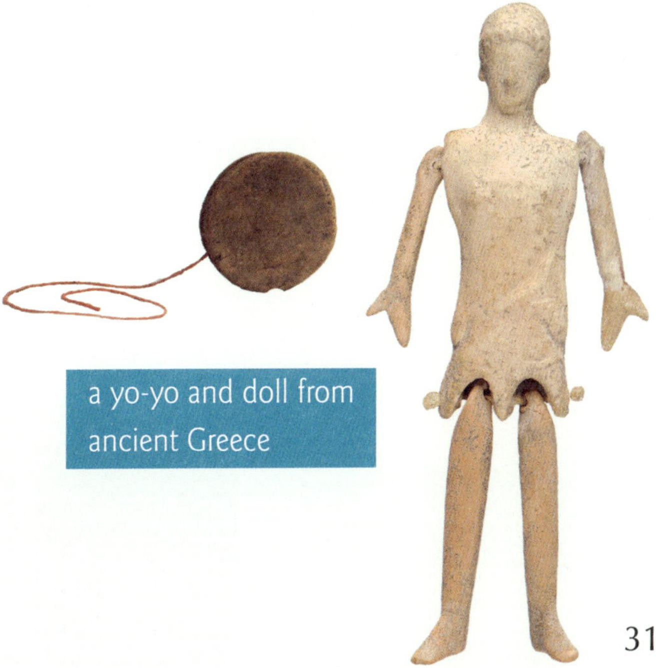

a yo-yo and doll from ancient Greece

Chapter 3
Ancient Egypt

If you stepped through time, and ended up with an ancient Egyptian family, you might not go to school. You'd be expected to learn to do your parents' work. You might help build a pyramid or learn how to be doctor. You'd wear a wraparound skirt or dress, unless you were a child-king. In that case you might have to wear a cloak made from the skin of a leopard, too!

A time traveller to ancient Egypt might see a scene like this.

The ancient Egyptian civilisation began about 5,000 years ago and lasted about 3,000 years. It is well-known for its pyramids. Like other civilisations, the ancient Egyptians began with people living beside a river. In an area of hot, dry deserts, the River Nile offered fresh water for drinking, growing food and washing.

The Step Pyramid is probably the oldest in the world.

The pyramids

Some of the most impressive ruins the ancient Egyptians left behind are pyramids. We know a lot about them, including why they were built. That's because of research by experts called Egyptologists, and also because of the Egyptians' own written records.

The largest pyramid is called the Great Pyramid. It's made from over two million huge blocks of stone and is as tall as a 45-storey block of flats. It used to be covered in a bright white stone that shimmered in the sunshine.

Imagine building a pyramid like this without modern machinery!

Pharaohs (rulers of ancient Egypt) had pyramids built to be their tombs. They were placed inside the pyramids after they died. The Great Pyramid became the tomb for a pharaoh called Khufu.

The remains of the Great Sphinx statue are close to the Great Pyramid. It's got the body of a lion and a human face. Some people think the face is meant to be Khufu's.

Inside the pyramids

The ancient Egyptians built secret entrances and tunnels in the pyramids, so that the tombs were hard to find. They had to keep their treasure-filled tombs safe from robbers. Unfortunately, robbers still managed to get in, so when people came to study the tombs, they were often empty.

the entrance to the Step Pyramid and a tunnel inside the Great Pyramid

Ready for the afterlife

The ancient Egyptians believed they could have another life after death. We know this from what they left behind. Wealthy ancient Egyptians wanted to make sure they'd have everything they needed for this afterlife, so they squeezed treasures and everyday objects into their tombs.

The remains of ancient Egyptian bodies still exist today. That's because the Egyptians had a way of keeping dead bodies in good condition, ready for the afterlife. These bodies are sometimes called mummified people. After preparing a dead body, they laid it in a sarcophagus (a kind of coffin, usually made of stone) inside their tomb.

remains of a broken sarcophagus in a pharaoh's tomb

Valley of the Queens

Some areas of ancient Egypt were covered in pyramids, temples and tombs.

One of these areas is called the Valley of the Queens. There are at least 75 female pharaohs buried here. One of the most magnificently decorated tombs belonged to Nefertari. The Egyptians' records show that she ruled alone, and could read and write. Few people could read and write at the time, and they were usually men.

Paintings in Nefertari's tomb show some of the many gods that ancient Egyptians believed in.

Nefertari's husband, Rameses the Great, was one of the most powerful pharaohs. He won lots of battles against an enemy empire and ordered temples to be built for himself and Nefertari.

Nefertari's temple: the massive statues show Nefertari, Rameses and their children

Statues of Rameses at the entrance to his temple

Valley of the Kings

There are over 60 tombs in the Valley of the Kings, many of which contained dead male pharaohs. One of the most famous tombs belonged to a very young pharaoh called Tutankhamun.

Unlike most of the other tombs, robbers didn't manage to steal much from Tutankhamun's. In 1922, when a historian discovered it under a heap of stones, the piles of treasure were still there. Hardly anyone had touched the treasure since Tutankhamun's burial, over 3,200 years before.

This photo shows the discovery of the tomb.

Child-pharaoh

Tutankhamun was about nine years old when he became ruler of ancient Egypt. Powerful people advised him because he was so young. He died aged about 18 years old.

One of the rooms in Tutankhamun's tomb contained a sarcophagus where his body lay.

The River Nile

Every year the River Nile flooded, leaving rich silt on its banks. The ancient Egyptians grew not only food in the soil but other plants, too. They grew cotton and flax for clothes, and also papyrus.

We know from ancient Egyptian wall paintings like these how important the Nile was.

Papyrus is a long, thin plant that grows in shallow water. The ancient Egyptians used it to make sheets that were a bit like paper for writing on.

Papyrus is also called the paper plant.

Experts examine ancient Egyptian writing on papyrus to learn more about the civilisation.

In 1960, governments started to build a dam to control the waters of the River Nile. The dam meant that the water would rise up over the Temples of Rameses and Nefertari! To save them, experts cut the temples into blocks and moved them to a higher, safer place. It took five years to move and rebuild the temples!

Chapter 4
Pictures, numbers and unsolved mysteries

Most of what we know about ancient Egyptian history, their rulers and their culture comes from their writing.

Picture writing

The ancient Egyptians' method of writing is one of the oldest in history. Instead of letters, it's made up of pictures and symbols, called hieroglyphs. It's been found on lots of different places, such as tomb walls and papyrus sheets.

hieroglyphs, carved onto a tomb wall

How do we know what it means?

We'd probably still be puzzling over the meaning of hieroglyphs if it weren't for a lucky find: the Rosetta Stone. This ancient stone, found over 200 years ago, shows the same text in three languages (hieroglyphs, an everyday ancient Egyptian language and Greek). After the stone's discovery, people who understood Greek could compare and work out the meaning of the hieroglyphs.

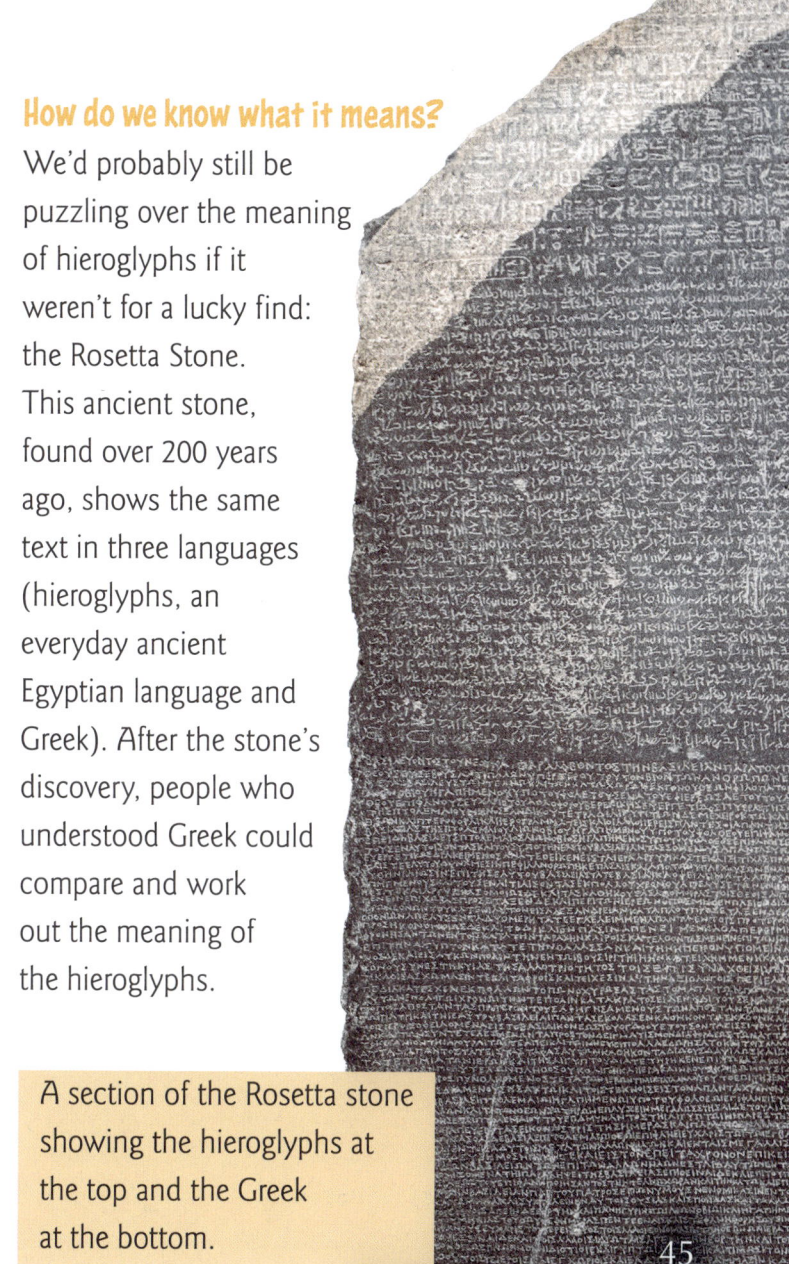

A section of the Rosetta stone showing the hieroglyphs at the top and the Greek at the bottom.

Boats and bread

Because the ancient Egyptians wanted to be well prepared for the afterlife, they put lots of personal belongings in their tombs. Many of these are now in museums. They give us even more of an idea of what life was like then.

Wooden model boats, often carrying a coffin, are sometimes found in tombs. They tell us what full-size boats on the River Nile might have looked like.

Combs, razors for shaving, and mirrors show that ancient Egyptians cared about their appearance. Clothes, like socks, sandals and robes, provide fashion clues. We even know more about what they ate because of food left in tombs, such as bread and dried fruit.

Ancient Egyptian paintings and carvings give us information, too. For example, they show that some people wore hair braids, hair extensions and wigs made from wool or human hair. They used a wax from bees to keep the hair in place.

Gold and treasure

The largest amount of ancient Egyptian treasure lay in Tutankhamun's tomb. Lots of the 5,398 items were made of gold, including a throne, Tutankhamun's funeral mask, and even the sandals on his body.

Tutankhamun's golden throne

Tutankhamun's mask is made from gold, with coloured glass and gemstones.

Other items placed in Tutankhamun's tomb for the afterlife include plenty of clothes, such as: 25 head coverings, 12 tunics, 28 gloves and four socks. There are lots of statues of servants, which suggest he expected to be well looked-after in his next life. He must have liked playing games, because a board game that's a bit like modern-day checkers or draughts was in the tomb, too.

Like most ancient Egyptians, Tutankhamun owned amulets: tiny carvings shaped like gods, animals or symbols. People thought these protected them. Amulets shaped like scarab beetles symbolised the sun god.

Fun and festivities

Ancient Egyptians left lots of evidence that they liked to have fun! As well as playing games, we know that they enjoyed sports and music.

Sports

Ancient Egyptian sports included athletics, long jump, weightlifting and wrestling. The River Nile offered a place for water sports like swimming, rowing and fishing.

Music

Ancient Egyptians played many different handmade instruments, including harps, flutes, and drums. They sang a lot, too.

This is a sistrum – it's shaped like a rattle but has jingles like a tambourine.

Feasts

Paintings and hieroglyphs tell us that the ancient Egyptians celebrated many festivals, with processions and feasts. Instead of plain foods, like bread and fruit, wealthy people offered more meat and different drinks at their festive feasts.

Thank you ancient Egyptians!

We can thank the ancient Egyptians for many things that we have in our modern world. As well as inventing one of the oldest forms of writing, they developed maths and medicines, too.

Numbers

Imagine trying to build a perfect pyramid. Every block must be exactly the right size and all the slopes must be angled to meet at the top. Papyrus books show that ancient Egyptians understood complex maths, so they could make exact measurements. They also worked out maths rules, like those we use today for measuring shapes.

They also came up with the first calendar with 365 days for each year. Their calendar also split the year into 12 divisions, like our 12 months.

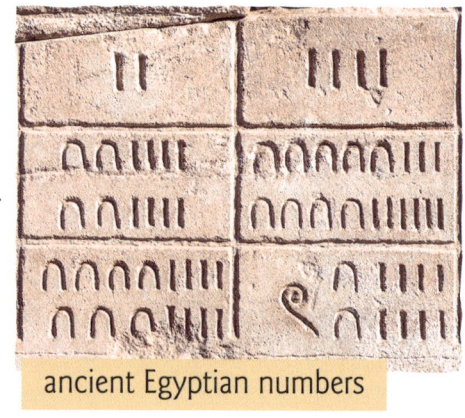
ancient Egyptian numbers

Medicine

Ancient Egyptian physicians or doctors (especially women) were the first to develop medical techniques that we use today. Examples are sedation (so people are asleep for operations) and antiseptics to stop infections.

These carvings show instruments the doctors used.

Unsolved mysteries

The missing queen

The tomb and body of the most important woman in ancient Egyptian history is missing!

Nefertiti was the wife of the powerful pharaoh Akhenaten, and Tutankhamun's stepmother. She had lots of titles, including 'Lady of all Women' and 'Lady of Grace'.

It's strange that there's no tomb for this important woman. However, Egyptologists think that hieroglyphs in Tutankhamun's tomb are a clue that she lies in a tomb nearby.

Nefertiti

A mysterious death

No one knows how or why the young pharaoh, Tutankhamun, died. One expert who examined his body thought someone might have murdered him. He thought he spotted damage from a blow to the head, but this later turned out to be a mistake.

Curse of the pharaohs
Lots of films are based on curses from pharaohs and mummified bodies. In fact, there's no evidence of ancient Egyptian curses.

The only signs on tombs tell people to keep out. This is understandable because they are places that should be respected, and they held lots of treasure.

Red Sea

River Nile

Upper Egypt

Valley of the Kings
Valley of the Queens

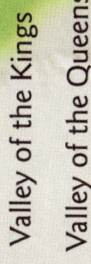

57

Ancient Egyptian animals

BONUS

Ancient Egyptians left lots of evidence showing how important animals were to them.

This is a statue of a cat goddess who represented the power of the sun.

This wall painting shows horses pulling chariots and a plough.

The pieces in this game are two types of dogs – jackals and hounds.

The snake on this pharaoh's headdress showed that the pharaoh was like a powerful god.

59

Chapter 5
The Inca empire

If you stepped 500 years back in time to the Inca empire, you would probably soon be digging the soil, planting seeds or leading llamas up and down mountainsides. (Inca children didn't have schools. They learnt everything from their older relatives.) Living in the mountains can be very cold but there is a good chance that you'd be given thick woolly clothes to wear.

Llama wool was woven into warm clothing.

At its strongest, the Inca empire was the biggest empire in the world. Like most empires, the Inca empire covered a large area, and it was ruled by a small group of powerful people.

Most people in the Inca empire worked on the land. They grew food and kept animals like llamas for meat, clothing and to carry things. Farmers lived in mud or stone houses. Powerful people, like royalty, lived in more comfortable homes in Cusco, the capital city of the Inca empire. Craftspeople and the army lived in cities too.

How the empire grew

The powerful Inca army was used to expand the empire. Each time it arrived somewhere, the people had a choice: join the Inca empire or try to fight back. Some people willingly joined because the Incas offered gifts and what seemed like a good deal. The Incas promised to provide them with food all year in exchange for work. The work included building, farming and being in the army.

People from different groups who had their own culture lived in the Inca empire. But the Inca rulers came from one group, called Quechua, and their language spread as the empire grew. Today, millions of people in South America speak different types of Quechua, passed down from the Incas.

The Wari
The Incas used what an earlier group of people called the Wari left behind. For example, they lengthened and strengthened some of the Wari's roads.

How did the Inca empire end?

Arguments between Inca rulers led to a deadly war. Also, explorers brought new diseases that killed many of the Incas. Finally, Spanish invaders came to steal the Incas' valuable gold. They killed the Inca ruler, and the empire ended in 1533.

a gold bird from the Inca empire

Machu Picchu

Machu Picchu is in the world's top ten most popular sites for tourists. Every year, 1.6 million people visit the ruined city (that's 4,300 visitors every day)!

When the winter got too cold, the Inca royals in Cusco travelled to Machu Picchu. They used Machu Picchu a bit like a holiday home. Fewer than a thousand people lived there, but when the royals arrived, they were kept very busy looking after them.

Machu Picchu had walkways, public squares, buildings like houses and temples, and a palace with a courtyard.

Temple of the Sun, Machu Picchu

How was it all built?

Machu Picchu is on a steep mountainside in the Andes, so workers had to cut thousands of steps for people to get to it. Tools that people left behind show that the Incas built Machu Picchu by hand. They didn't have wheels or carts for rolling the rock around, or strong metals like steel for cutting. They used sticks, knives, axes and chisels to dig and to shape stone.

Earthquakes

Machu Picchu is in an earthquake zone so the area is often rocked by movements in the earth. Earthquakes can collapse buildings, so how has Machu Picchu survived for so long?

The Inca builders cut the stone blocks so they fitted very tightly together, without any sticking mixture like mud (or today's cement). When an earthquake hit, the stones just rocked and wobbled, and then slipped back into position afterwards. The builders also tilted some of the walls, so that they leant towards the mountainside. This made them stronger and less likely to collapse, too.

The stones fit so tightly, you can't slip a sheet of paper between them.

An Inca greenhouse?

At Moray in the Andes, there are three giant, bowl-like hollows dug into the mountainside. One hollow is so deep that you could bury a ten-storey building in it! The sides of the hollows are shaped in a series of steps, called terraces.

hand-built terraces

The lowest terraces are much warmer than those higher up. The Incas used these lowest terraces like a greenhouse to grow plants that would usually die in the cold mountain air.

Roads and bridges

The Incas built about 40,000 kilometres of roads. That's long enough to stretch all around the world! They built the whole road network by hand. To make sure roads lasted, they added steps and holes to let water drain away, and used local stone that wouldn't crack in the ice or snow. While modern roads are sometimes washed away, Inca roads are still here after 600 years!

Inca roads cross all kinds of landscapes, from steep mountains to rocky deserts.

The roads kept the empire together. The Incas didn't have horses, so they had to travel on foot. However, the roads meant that teams of people could carry a message nearly 3,000 kilometres, from Cusco to Quito, in just five days. That's the same distance as 70 marathons!

Lots of tiny roads led off this main network that linked two main cities.

Straw bridges

To cross steep valleys and rivers, the Incas built bridges made from straw. This Inca bridge survives because local people take turns to mend it using Inca bridge-building skills. These skills have been handed down through the generations for 500 years.

Chapter 6
Food, gold and missing treasure

Scientists studied soil and plants from the 'greenhouse' terraces at Moray. This showed that the Incas grew many different plants on different levels of the terraces. They even developed new plants, including hundreds of different types of potatoes.

Controlling water
The Incas made sure their crops survived in a drought. At Moray, they built channels to carry water to the terraces.

Channels controlled the flow of water.

Food all year round

Food quickly rots unless it is carefully stored or preserved. To store enough food, like corn, to eat through the year, the Incas built tall storehouses where cool breezes kept the food fresh.

To preserve food, the Incas also used a process called freeze-drying. Today, we use machines to freeze-dry food. The Incas used the weather. They laid potatoes out to freeze at night. When the sun warmed the potatoes in the day, they squashed the water out. After repeating the process, the potatoes were dry enough to store for years.

the ruins of 27 storehouses high in the Andes

Gold

Inca people believed that gold is the sun's sweat, and silver is the moon's tears. Because they worshipped a sun god and believed that their ruler had descended from him, gold had a special value.

Inca gold, showing the sun god

The Incas dug gold from the mountains and hammered it into jewellery, figurines and everyday objects. However, few Inca gold items are left because the Spanish invaders stole and melted them to sell the gold. Some survived for archaeologists to find, buried in graves or amongst Inca ruins.

The Festival of the Sun
The Inca Festival of the Sun, Inti Raymi, took place around 24th June each year. It marked the start of planting crops. Today, the Incas' descendants still celebrate this important day in honour of their ancestors.

People wear traditional Inca clothes at the Inti Raymi festival.

Cloth and figurines

Woven cloth

The Incas treasured the cloth they made – perhaps more than gold. The finest cloths were woven from alpaca or llama wool. The king and his family wore tunics of particular woven designs, which probably had special meanings.

Offerings

The Incas respected the land, so they carved small wood and stone figurines to bury as offerings to Mother Earth. Many of these figurines look like alpaca because these animals were so important to them.

carved alpaca

After death

Inca tombs show how much they cared about people who had died. After death, people's bodies were often wrapped in leather or cloth to preserve them, and then buried with personal belongings.

an entrance to a royal tomb in Machu Picchu

Thanks to the Incas

Today, we have a lot to thank the Incas for. The Inca farmers' use of terraces teaches us how to work with a steep landscape and grow foods on terraces. Road engineers learn from the Incas' lasting roads. Other amazing things include the following.

A living language

The language spoken by the Incas, called Quechua, is still spoken in western parts of South America.

Did you know that some English words come from the Quechuan (*KETCH-wuhn*) language?

poncho   puma   llama   condor

Foods

Thanks to the Incas' experimental farming, we have lots of nutritious foods, including corn, beans and potatoes.

Weaving – a living tradition

Ancient Inca weaving skills are still used to make clothes and blankets today. Weavers living high in the Andes mountains still share and develop these skills, helping to keep them alive for future generations.

women spinning wool, ready to weave

Unsolved mysteries

The Incas left behind a lot of mysteries, which experts still hope to solve.

Inca records

The Incas didn't have a written language, but they kept records using a different system: knotted string cords, called quipu. The cords might have been used to record numbers, or even stories or songs. No one has fully worked out their meaning, although the colours and number of knots are probably important.

Machu Picchu

No one knows for sure why the Incas abandoned Machu Picchu. Perhaps a long drought meant that even with careful farming their mountainside crops died. Also, there's still a lot to find out about Machu Picchu's Temple of the Sun. The position of its windows and altar (a table for worship) suggest that the Incas built it to honour Inti, their sun god. Some people think that the Incas used the temple as an observatory, where they measured the sun's position and worked out when to start planting crops.

an Inca quipu

Hidden treasure?

Another Inca mystery is based on a legend about a hoard of golden treasure.

The hoard

When the Inca empire began to fall, the invading Spanish captured the Inca king. The Spanish commander said he would let the king go in exchange for a roomful of gold. After most of the gold had been delivered, the commander broke his promise and killed the king. The Incas buried the rest of the treasure in a secret cave.

Spanish commander: Francisco Pizarro

the Inca king: Atahualpa

A Spaniard found the treasure 50 years later and became very rich. When he died, he left information on where to find the rest of it. But hundreds of years passed before a Canadian treasure hunter called Barth Blake found the remaining gold. Barth couldn't carry it all, so he left on a boat, planning to go back. But he fell (or was pushed) overboard into the sea, along with the treasure's location.

The legend says the gold is somewhere near the black cross on the map.

Food

By looking at what lost civilisations left behind, we can learn about what they ate.

Experts found Indus Valley pots and in them were tiny remains. These turned out to be the oldest known curry! This is a modern aubergine curry.

Decorations, like the corn on this Inca pot, show what food they ate.

Wall paintings show ancient Egyptian food crops.

This ancient Egyptian model shows how they shaped and baked their bread.

The oldest recipes, written on clay tablets from Mesopotamia, include soups, stews and pies.

Are these civilisations really lost?

Many people think that civilisations aren't completely 'lost'. In lots of ways, they appear in our lives today.

town planning and drains from the Indus Valley people

lots of different kinds of potatoes from the Incas

All ancient civilisations inspire artists and writers.

the 365 days calendar
from the ancient Egyptians

About the author

How do you go about writing a non-fiction book like this?

First, I note down all the reasons why I want to write the book. For this book, I listed all the awesome facts that I already knew about these amazing civilisations. Next, I do the research. For this book, I read about the new discoveries made by archaeologists and scientists. After tidying up my research notes, I can start to write the first page!

Liz Miles

What's your favourite thing about writing books?

My favourite thing is the magic of it. You can focus on an idea or subject that excites you and spend days getting lost in it. Then, at the end, you find that you've written a book!

If you could time travel to any of these lost civilisations, which would you visit and why?

I'd travel to ancient Egypt because I really can't work out how they managed to build those giant pyramids without cranes or other machinery!

What's the most interesting or surprising thing you learnt while writing this book?

The most interesting and exciting thing is the unsolved mysteries! I'd love to be an archaeologist and help solve them. The detective work must be fascinating.

What do you think are the best things these lost civilisations left behind?
I think that we can still learn a lot from the Moray 'greenhouse'. Using the Incas' ideas, we could grow lots of good food. The Incas managed to grow lots of food in a difficult landscape. But they didn't interfere with nature in a big way or use chemicals like weed-killers.

Are there any other lost civilisations you think are interesting?
I find the ancient civilisation that lived on what we now call Easter Island fascinating. They left behind giant statues, and no one knows how the people managed to make them, or what happened to the civilisation itself. They left behind an island of secrets! Also, I'm very interested in two of the most famous ancient civilisations: the ancient Greeks and the ancient Romans. They left behind lots of art and architecture to admire. Their myths fill my imagination and inspire lots of new stories.

What do you hope readers will get out of this book?
I hope readers feel grateful to these civilisations. I came to realise that they left behind lots of wonderful things — including buttons, games, and how to build strong walls and roads! They achieved so much without any of the machinery or technology that we have.

Book chat

> Had you heard of any of these places or people before reading the book?

> If you could time travel to any of these lost civilisations, which would you visit and why?

> Which of the things the civilisations have left behind do you think are the most interesting?

What was the most surprising or interesting thing you learnt while reading this book?

What do you think are the things we'd leave behind for people 500 years in the future?

If you could ask the author anything, what would you ask?

Who would you recommend this book to and why?

If you had to think of a new title for this book, what would you choose?

Do you have a favourite picture in the book? Why do you like it?

If you had to give the author one piece of advice to make the book better, what would you say?

Would you like to read another book about lost civilisations?

If you could learn more about one of these three civilisations, which would you choose and why?

If you could talk to someone from each of these three civilisations, what would you ask?

Book challenge:
What three things would you leave behind in a time capsule for future experts to find?

Published by Collins
An imprint of HarperCollins*Publishers*

The News Building
1 London Bridge Street
London
SE1 9GF
UK

Macken House
39/40 Mayor Street Upper
Dublin 1
D01 C9W8
Ireland

© HarperCollins*Publishers* Limited 2025

10 9 8 7 6 5 4 3 2 1

ISBN 978-0-00-874643-8

All rights reserved. No part of this publication may be reproduced, stored in a retrieval system, or transmitted in any form by any means, electronic, mechanical, photocopying, recording or otherwise, without the prior written permission of the Publisher or a licence permitting restricted copying in the United Kingdom issued by the Copyright Licensing Agency Ltd, 5th Floor, Shackleton House, 4 Battle Bridge Lane, London SE1 2HX.

Without limiting the author's and publisher's exclusive rights, any unauthorised use of this publication to train generative artificial intelligence (AI) technologies is expressly prohibited. HarperCollins also exercise their rights under Article 4(3) of the Digital Single Market Directive 2019/790 and expressly reserve this publication from the text and data mining exception.

British Library Cataloguing-in-Publication Data A catalogue record for this publication is available from the British Library.

Download the teaching notes and word cards to accompany this book at:
http://littlewandle.org.uk/signupfluency/

Get the latest Collins Big Cat news at
collins.co.uk/collinsbigcat

Author: Liz Miles
Illustrator: Martin Sanders (Beehive Illustration)
Publisher: Laura White
Product managers: Caroline Green and Holly Woolnough
Series editor: Charlotte Raby
Development editor: Catherine Baker
Commissioning editor: Caroline Green
Project manager: Emily Hooton
Copyeditor: Sally Byford
Proofreader: Catherine Dakin
Cover designer: Sarah Finan
Typesetter: 2Hoots Publishing Services Ltd
Production controller: Katharine Willard

Printed in the UK.

MIX
Paper | Supporting responsible forestry
FSC™ C007454

This book contains FSC™ certified paper and other controlled sources to ensure responsible forest management.

For more information visit: www.harpercollins.co.uk/green

Made with responsibly sourced paper and vegetable ink

Scan to see how we are reducing our environmental impact.

Acknowledgements
The publishers gratefully acknowledge the permission granted to reproduce the copyright material in this book. Every effort has been made to trace copyright holders and to obtain their permission for the use of copyright material. The publishers will gladly receive any information enabling them to rectify any error or omission at the first opportunity.

Front cover Oleh Ustinov/Shutterstock, p5 Sabena Jane Blackbird/Alamy, pp6–7 DEA / G. NIMATALLAH/Getty Images, p12 Travel India/Alamy, p13 Christine Osborne Pictures/Alamy, p14r Heritage Image Partnership Ltd/Alamy, p15 robertharding/Alamy, p17b Suzuki Kaku/Alamy, p18 robertharding/Alamy, p19t Suzuki Kaku/Alamy, p19b Angelo Hornak/Getty Images, p20 Roger Wood/Getty Images, p23t Angelo Hornak/Alamy, p23b Dragan Nikolic/Alamy, p24l Suzuki Kaku/Alamy, p24c De Agostini/Getty Images, p24r World History Archive/Alamy, p25 Heritage Image Partnership Ltd/Alamy, p26t Suzuki Kaku/Alamy, p26b World History Archive/Alamy, p30t The Print Collector/Alamy, p30b Suzuki Kaku/Alamy, p31bl Gary Todd/Wikimedia Commons, p31br Science History Images/Alamy, p37 robertharding/Alamy, p39t Design Pics Inc/Alamy, p40 David Cole/Alamy, p46 The Print Collector/Alamy, p49 spatuletail/Shutterstock, p51 De Agostini/Getty Images, p53 LightRocket/Getty Images, p58t De Agostini/Getty Images, p62 Peter Horree/Alamy, p72t Deco/Alamy, p72b Alistair Laming/Alamy, p73t J Marshall - Tribaleye Images/Alamy, p73b Penta Springs Limited/Alamy, p75b Grant Rooney Premium/Alamy, p78l Corbis/Getty Images, p83c De Agostini/Getty Images, p83b GRANGER - Historical Picture Archive/Alamy, back cover tr Vadim Petrakov/Shutterstock, bl mapimarf/Shutterstock, br Deco/Alamy.

All other photos Shutterstock.